Sets

Sorting into Groups

by Michele Koomen

Consultant:
Deborah S. Ermoian
Mathematics Faculty
Phoenix College
Phoenix, Arizona

Bridgestone Books
an imprint of Capstone Press
Mankato, Minnesota

Bridgestone Books are published by Capstone Press
151 Good Counsel Drive, P.O. Box 669, Mankato, Minnesota 56002
http://www.capstone-press.com

Library of Congress Cataloging-in-Publication Data
Koomen, Michele.
    Sets: sorting into groups/by Michele Koomen.
    p. cm.—(Exploring math)
    Includes bibliographical references and index.
    ISBN 0-7368-0822-1
    1. Set theory—Juvenile literature. [1. Set theory.] I. Title. II. Series.
QA248 .K62 2001
511.3'22—dc21

00-010564

Summary: Simple text, photographs, and illustrations introduce the concept of sorting
    objects into sets and subsets, including real-world examples of sorting.

Editorial Credits
Tom Adamson, editor; Lois Wallentine, product planning editor; Linda Clavel, designer;
    Katy Kudela, photo researcher

Photo Credits
Capstone Press/CG Book Printers, cover
Gregg Andersen, 16–17, 18, 20, 21

1 2 3 4 5 6 06 05 04 03 02 01

44701648
3-22-00

Table of Contents

Sorting into Groups

It is hard to tell what objects you have when they are jumbled together. You sometimes need to sort objects.

Sorting is putting objects into groups that have something in common. Each group is called a set.

5

Sorting by Color

You can sort these candies by color. The candies in each set are alike because they are the same color. You can sort the red candies into a red set. The yellow candies go in a yellow set. What other color sets can you make?

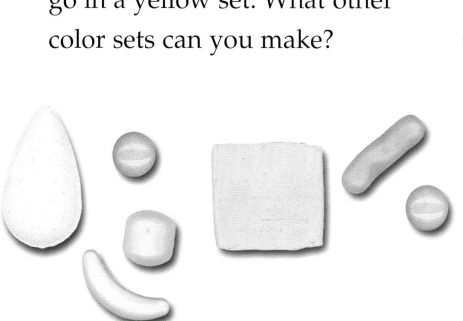

8

Sorting by Size

You can sort candies by size. Large candies go in one set. Small candies make up another set. What other size sets can you make?

Sorting by Shape

You can sort objects by shape. Round candies make up one set. Square and rectangular candies fit into another set. Other candies have odd shapes. How would you sort them into sets?

11

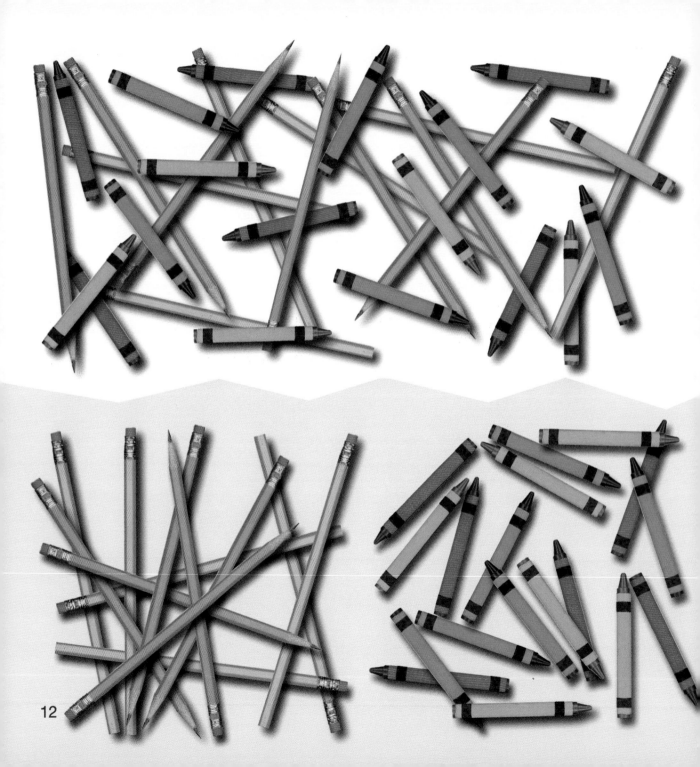

Sorting Crayons and Pencils

You can sort these crayons and pencils into two sets. You have one set of crayons and one set of pencils. Each set can be sorted again. How can you sort the set of crayons into smaller groups?

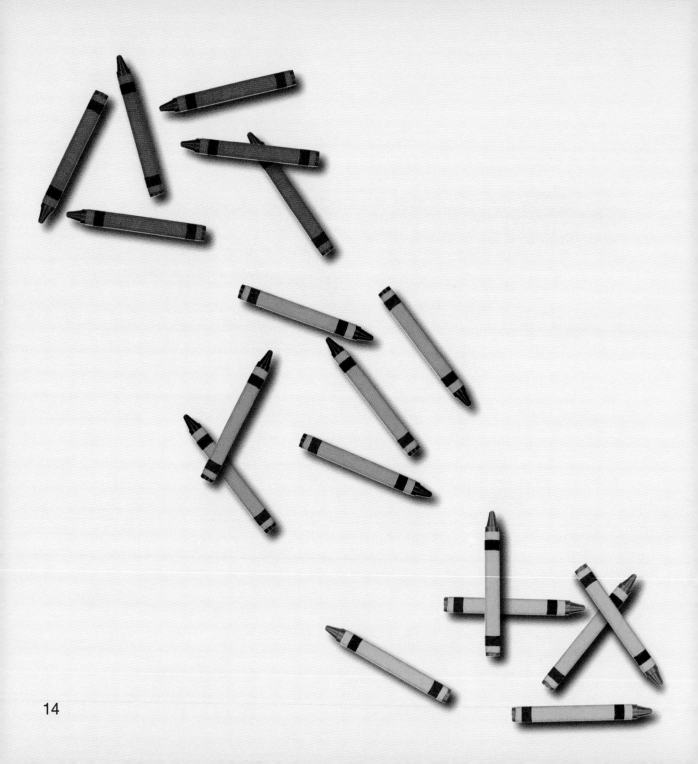

Subsets

You can sort the crayons by color. These new groups are subsets. A subset is a group that is part of a set. The group of red crayons is a subset of the set of crayons. The group of blue crayons is another subset.

ERS

YELLOW
ZUCCHINI
3 FOR $1.09
35¢ EAC

ZUCC
3 FOR
35¢

Sorting at the Market

Workers sort products to sell at the market. You can find zucchini in one place. You can find peppers in another place. Different types of peppers are sorted into different baskets. Sorting food at the market makes it easy for customers to find what they want.

← NONFICTION

← MAGAZINES

REFERENCE DESK ↓

SK ↓

FICTION →

BUSI ESS
RESOURCES

Sorting at the Library

Books in the library are sorted into sets. Nonfiction books are in one area. Fiction books are sorted in another area. Sorting at the library makes it easier to find books on different topics.

Subsets at the Library

Books can be sorted into subsets too. These shelves have a set of animal books. Books about dogs are a subset of the animal books.

Books about horses make up
another subset.

Hands On: Sorting Shoes

Almost anything can be sorted into sets. You can practice sorting with shoes.

What You Need

A large group of friends
Shoes

What You Do

1. Form a large circle.
2. Everyone takes off one shoe and places it in the center of the circle.
3. This group of shoes is one set. Notice the different ways the shoes are alike.
4. Sort the shoes by color. Count how many shoes are in each subset. How many color subsets can you make?
5. Now sort the shoes by how you put them on. Count how many shoes have laces, have fabric fasteners, or slip on. Each of these groups is a subset.

Are there other ways you can sort shoes?

Words to Know

fiction (FIK-shuhn)—stories that are not real

nonfiction (NON-fik-shuhn)—writing that is about real things, people, and events

set (SET)—a group of objects that have something in common

sort (SORT)—to arrange or separate objects into groups

subset (SUHB-set)—a group of objects that is part of a set

zucchini (zoo-KEE-nee)—a vegetable with smooth dark green or yellow skin

Read More

Bryant-Mole, Karen. *Sorting*. Mortimer's Math. Milwaukee: Gareth Stevens, 2000.

Murphy, Stuart J. *Dave's Down-to-Earth Rock Shop.* MathStart. New York: HarperCollins, 2000.

Patilla, Peter. *Sorting*. Math Links. Des Plaines, Ill.: Heinemann Library, 2000.

Internet Sites

Ask Dr. Math
http://mathforum.com/dr.math
Figure This! Math Challenges for Families
http://www.figurethis.org
MathSteps
http://www.eduplace.com/math/mathsteps/index.html

Index